Dwayne's Guitar Lessons
Presents:

Learn To Play Rhythm Guitar

By

Dwayne Jenkins

Introduction

The great thing about learning to play an instrument like the guitar is it builds self-confidence. Learn To Play Rhythm Guitar is a training guide that will do just that. Along with teaching you the inner workings of playing rhythm guitar.

But for that to happen, you must stick with it. Patience and self-discipline are not things that merely happen, they are things that develop over time. This is done through repetition of study, practice, and daily application.

Learning to play rhythm guitar can benefit you in many other ways as well. It can provide a relaxing hobby. It can unlock the mysteries of your favorite songs, and it allows you to even play those songs.

Once you have the basics down, you can apply that to other stringed instruments that you might want to play in the future. Although I recommend you work at learning one at a time so as not to lose focus.

Rhythm guitar is a great thing to learn because it sets the foundation for music. No matter if it's music you listen to and want to learn how to play, or music you might want to write yourself and share with the world.

In this comprehensive course, you will learn the inner workings of rhythm guitar. Like what type of guitar to play. How to form chords. How to strum and create rhythm, How to establish timing, and the basics of reading guitar notation.

A helpful training guide that has been designed to give you a clear and concise step-by-step method of study. It will propel you forward and you will be having fun in no time. Even if you have no previous musical knowledge.

Learn to play rhythm guitar is loaded with pictures diagrams and notation for productive learning. Follow the steps and you will build a foundation that all future studies can easily stand on. Which unfortunately is what a lot of guitar players miss.

Once your goals are set, and your focus is tuned in, you will be ready to head down the trail of learning. This informative method book will get you there in no time. Just follow it like a map to a hidden treasure. Good luck and have fun.

Dwayne Jenkins

Table of Contents

Chapter 1 Getting Started

Lesson 1: Guitar anatomy

What kind of guitar is best for playing rhythm? Well, when it comes to the guitar, there are many to choose from. You can play an acoustic guitar, or you can play an electric guitar. It is really up to you and what you prefer.

All guitars are roughly the same. But they do differ in look size, weight, and tone. Especially if you compare an electric to an acoustic. But most acoustics are similar, as well as most electrics. You just need to find what's best for you.

What is great about the guitar compared to other instruments is that it comes in a variety of sizes, shapes, and colors, so it is easy to find one that fits your personality. You'll know when you've found the right one because It will just say "Hi, pick me".

And if you've never played the guitar before or know nothing about music, no worries. Just follow the step-by-step method laid out in this book and you will see quick results. I know you will because it is the same method I used.

So let's look at the guitar and get familiar with the anatomy of the instrument.

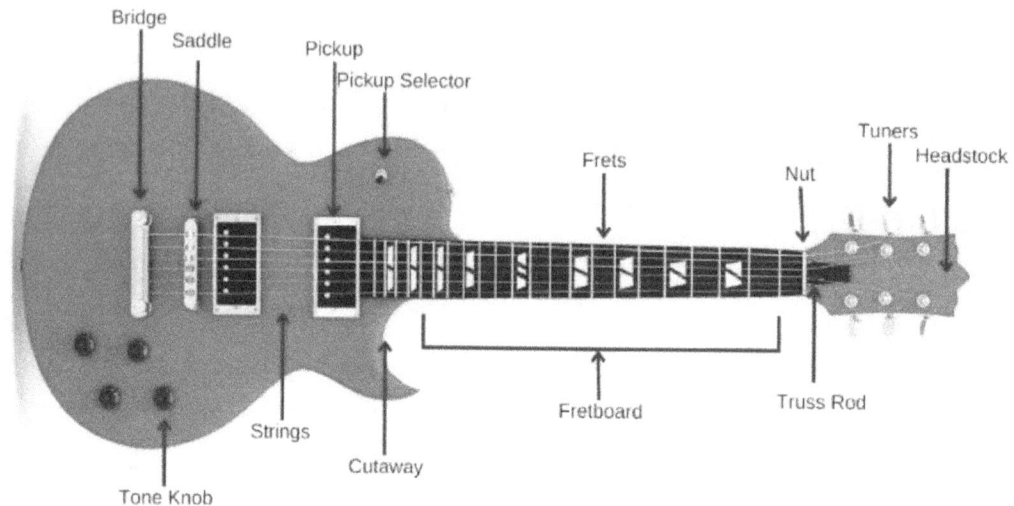

Here is an example of an electric guitar. This is the type that is most common when playing rhythm, so this is the type we will be learning about in this training.

If you prefer an acoustic guitar, I recommend you check out my book Learn To Play Acoustic For Beginners.

Headstock: This is the top of the guitar where the tuning pegs are located.

Tuners: These are what hold the strings and tune the guitar.

Nut: This is what holds the strings in place when it's played.

Frets: These are the wires that separate the fretboard into playing positions.

Fretboard: This is the front part of the neck, where you will place your fingers to form guitar chords.

Truss rod: This is a rod that goes through the neck to keep it straight.

Pickups: Magnets that pickup the vibration of the strings to create sound on an electric guitar.

Selector switch: This selects which pickup to use, as each one provides a different sound

Tone knobs: This allows you to adjust the sound of the instrument and control the volume.

Saddle: This is what transfers the string vibration to the wood of the guitar.

Bridge: This is where the strings are held in place on the body of the guitar.

4

Lesson 2: Guitar posture

When it comes to playing the guitar, you can play in two positions. Well, maybe more if you're getting a little crazy with it, but we'll save that for after we learn to play it. The two most common ways are sitting or standing.

I recommend for learning, to start with playing it sitting down. This will make it easier for you to get used to the instrument. Once you get a few chords down and feel a bit comfortable with it, you can then try standing up.

The guitar is shaped a certain way to make it more comfortable to play. Its design has been engineered to be comfortable sitting down with the curve underneath the body. This will allow you to rest it on your leg as you play it.

What is great about guitars, is they come in different sizes and shapes. So you can find one that fits you. Just make sure you can reach the whole fretboard and it is comfortable when you hold it.

Lesson 3: Hand positioning

What is great about learning an instrument like the guitar is that it becomes an extension of you and your personality. As you continue down your journey, you will discover what works for you and your style of playing.

You use all teaching as guidance. Instruction on how to do it. You then make adjustments along the way that fit you and how you prefer to approach the guitar. This is what makes it the best instrument in the world.

Use this method book and its lessons to show you the ropes and teach you what you need to know. You then learn from other books, or private lessons from teachers or friends. As you do so, you will discover and develop your style.

Your fretboard hand

With this hand, you will form and play guitar chords. These will be part of the foundation of songs. Your development of this hand is vitally important. Be sure to put in the time and effort as it will serve you well.

6

Here is a good example of how your hand should look.

As you can see, your thumb is on the top and your fingers are curled around the front. This is how you'll form a chord. The guitar neck is shaped this way for this particular reason. In this example, the chord being formed is an E major.

Most guitar chords will be formed on multiple strings. This is what can make it a bit challenging at first. But as time goes on and your fingers develop, it'll get easier. But it will take some time so be sure to put in the effort.

This is the development of the fretboard hand. It will take time because your hands and fingers must get used to holding down metal wires on a piece of wood. Which is exactly what you are doing with the guitar. Acoustic, or electric.

Picking hand development

The picking hand is what will create a rhythm for the chords that your fretboard hand forms. They will need to work in harmony with each other for the guitar to create music. This hand will either strum the chords or pick them individually.

Below is an example of how your picking hand should look.

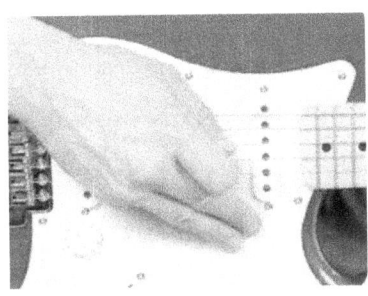

Notice how the arm is over the body and the hand is above the strings around the middle of the guitar body. The thumb and index finger will hold the pick and the whole hand will work to control the vibration of the strings when being played.

As I stated before, everyone plays a bit differently, and over time you will develop your style, but for now, do as instructed for the best outcome of your performance.

When strumming chords, be sure to keep your wrist loose. Keep your fingers close to the body of the guitar and be sure that the guitar is comfortable in your hands. You should not have to strain to play it.

When you strum the chords you will use a pick to brush across the strings. Keep your arm close to the body and make sure you can reach everything with ease. Being comfortable is highly important when playing the guitar.

How you approach the instrument will make a huge difference in the music that comes out as you play. I will show you what is best, but over time you will discover little things that will help develop your style.

Go through these few lessons and make sure you fully understand how to hold the guitar and what each hand is supposed to be doing. This will set the foundation. Once you have that down, we will then learn how to get it in tune.

Without it being in tune, no good music can be produced with the guitar. So make sure to learn this lesson and learn it well.

Lesson 4: Tuning up

To create music out of the guitar all six strings must be in harmony with each other. Meaning they must all be at a certain pitch. Each string is different and it must be learned at what pitch each one needs to be at about the others.

This is what allows it to be in tune and allows it to produce music that people enjoy listening to. The best way to tune your guitar is with an electronic tuner. These are easy to use and readily available.

But before we can get it tuned up, we must learn the names of all six strings. This is what we will tune each string to and get the guitar to sound good when we play it.

All 6 strings on the guitar

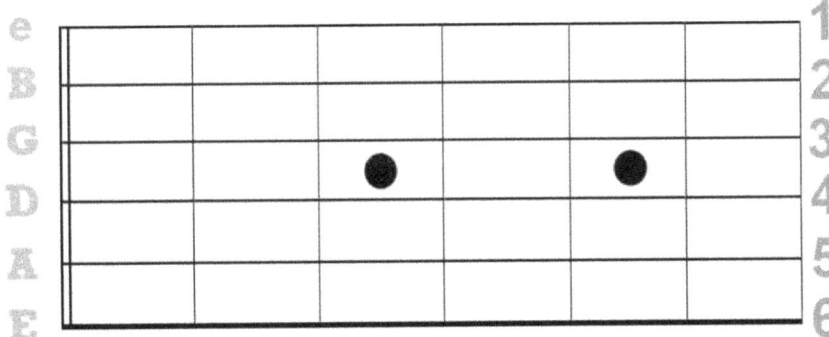

As you can see from the picture, each string has a different name. Make sure to remember these string names. You'll also notice that two strings have the same name. Which means you only have to learn the names of five strings.

Also, notice that the sixth string is on the bottom of the diagram, but it will be on the top of your guitar. This is very important to remember for the lesson on reading sheet music. Study this diagram as it will help you in future lessons.

Once you learn the names of the strings, you can then proceed to make sure they are tuned correctly. Here are a couple of tuner examples to use.

Clip-on tuners are very popular

This type of tuner is a great option. It clips onto your headstock and has a nice big display for the strings. They come in different colors and are easy to use. Highly recommended.

The reason why these are so popular is because they are small, portable, and can be used for both electric and acoustic guitars. They can be kept on the headstock, or stored in your guitar bag when not in use.

Some even come with guitars you buy online, which makes them even more popular. Another type of tuner that is very handy, is the tuner app.

Popular Guitar Tuner App.

Everything nowadays has an app. So why not a guitar tuner app? There are many apps to choose from. The GuitarTuna app is the one I use. It's very popular and easy to use, and you can download it on your phone for free.

Tuner apps are nice because they offer more than just a tuner. You might have to pay a small monthly fee, but they have options to help improve your learning.

Whether you choose the clip-on type of tuner or the app type of tuner, it doesn't matter. They are both great options to get the job done. And remember, having the guitar in tune is what's most important.

To remember the string names, you can use an acronym to help you remember. There are two that I like.

1.) From 6th to 1st: Eddie Ate Dynamite GoodBye, Eddie.
2.) From 1st to 6th. Easter Bunnies Go Dancing After Easter.

Either one of these will work to remember the string names. Just decide which one works best for you.

Remember, knowing the string names and numbers will allow you to tune it correctly. This is one of the most important lessons to learn. So study it well.

It is what's needed to make the guitar sound good when you learn to play it.

Lesson 5: Chapter 1 Quiz

In this lesson, I have provided you with a simple quiz to test your knowledge of what you have learned, or not learned within this chapter. If you miss something or don't know it, don't worry. Just go back and find it in the lessons.

This is a great way to make sure that you know the material and are ready for the next chapter. Have fun and good luck.

Q: What is the guitar anatomy?

A: _____

Q: What two ways can you play the guitar?

A: _____

Q: What is the function of your fretboard hand?

A: _____

Q: What is the function of your picking hand?

A: _____

Q: What is the function of the truss rod?

A: _____

14

Q: What is the nut designed to do?

A: _____

Q: What is the function of the pickups?

A: _____

Q: What is the function of the selector switch?

A: _____

Q: How many strings are on the guitar?

A: _____

Q: What are the two acronyms for remembering them?

A: _____

Q: What is a clip-on tuner?

A: _____

Q: What is a guitar tuner App?

A; _____

Q: Why is tuning the guitar so important?

A; _____

Know the answers to these questions, and know them well.
These lessons will set the foundation of your guitar education.
The better your foundation, the better your guitar playing.

Chapter 1 Summary

In this first chapter, we have covered some of the basics. This will set the foundation for all future studies. From this book and other books, you will learn from in the future.

We first looked at the guitar anatomy. We learn the parts and how they allow the instrument to function. When you learn this, it gives you a better understanding and appreciation for the instrument.

We then learned about how to hold the guitar. We learned that there are mainly two ways to play it. Sitting down, or standing up. Both are beneficial in their way and I recommend learning both. But for now, try sitting down.

We then looked at hand positioning. Both hands will be used. The fretboard hand forms and holds the chords. And the picking hand to create the rhythm through strumming the strings, or picking the strings individually.

And the most important thing lesson learned in this chapter, is how to tune the guitar. This will be mastered by learning the string names and being able to use the correct guitar tuner to get them tuned to pitch. Learn this lesson well.

16

Chapter 2 Natural Chords

Lesson 6: Guitar chord charts

Before we get into learning to form guitar chords, we want to learn to read guitar chord charts. These charts will allow you to remember how the chords are formed once you learn them. As well as make it easier to learn new chords later.

These are box diagrams that allow us to visually see how the chords are shaped. They are a very popular way to read guitar chords.

Here is a chord chart example:

This is a diagram that will show you the strings as well as the fret position of the chord. This works great because all the natural chords we learn will be played within the first few frets.

The diagram consists of vertical and horizontal lines. The vertical lines represent the 6 guitar strings with the low E string on the left and the high E string on the right.

The horizontal lines represent the nut and the first five frets. This is where most open chords are played. If chords are formed further up the fretboard, then a number will be presented on the left to indicate this.

The thing about chord charts that you need to remember, is that they show the guitar facing upward. Not sideways like you normally play it. This can make them a bit confusing to learn at first. But it will get easier over time. Just work at it.

Reading any type of musical sheet music can be a bit daunting at first, but if you take it one step at a time, you will discover how it can be very beneficial to your guitar playing.

Remember, music is a language. And you are learning to read and understand it. This is the type of skill that will give you an edge over other guitar players. As most play by ear.

But it is like learning anything else. It takes time and patience. Repetition of looking at the chord charts over and over again and getting it firmly grasped in your mind how it looks and how the chord is formed.

With dedicated time and commitment, you will be able to read any chord chart that is put in front of you. And with daily guitar practice, you will be able to form and play the chord that is presented with confidence.

Lesson 7: E minor & E major

The easiest chord to form on the guitar is the E minor chord. It requires two fingers on two strings, both on the 2nd fret. This is the easiest open chord to play and will set the foundation for all other chords that follow it.

E minor

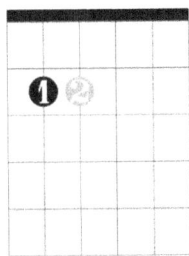

When we look at the diagram above we can see that we have two numbers. These will represent your fingers. Your index and second finger. They will be on the fifth and fourth strings on the 2nd fret.

Remember, the guitar is facing upward and the vertical lines represent the guitar strings with the 6th being to the far left. With the horizontal lines representing the frets. Make sure to fully understand this concept.

Now, if we add another note to the shape, we can form the E major chord. This chord will just be called E. All major chords will be identified this way.

E

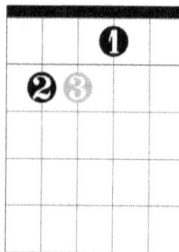

As you can see, we just added a note to the previous chord and now have the E major chord. We'll have to reposition our fingers. Or get used to playing the E minor with the second and third fingers. Then we can just add the index for the major.

I recommend you work at forming it both ways. You never know what chord is going to come next in a song. So being able to form a chord in multiple ways can be very beneficial to your playing.

Your first step will be to form chords. Your second will be able to switch between them. Your third step will be to put them together in a sequence to form chord progressions. Which is the essence of playing rhythm.

The E minor and E major are presented first because they are not too difficult to form and are very popular in many songs. Plus they will set the foundation for additional chords we will learn in upcoming lessons.

Lesson 8: A minor & C major

Next, we will learn the A minor and C major chords. These come next because of their ease of form and their popularity in many songs.

A minor

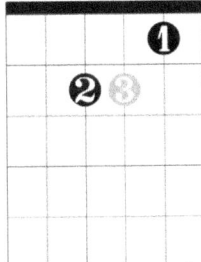

As you can see, this chord is the same shape as the E major. The only difference is that we move everything down a string. This gives us the A minor chord.

You want to look at chords in shapes. The reason for this is that you will notice over time, that a lot of them have the same or similar shapes. This makes them easier to learn.

The A minor is a very popular song in many songs and is considered a foundation type of chord. That is why it is presented third. Practice going back and forth between the A minor and E major chords.

We now learn one of the most important chords. The C major chord. I say important because you can get other chords quite easily from here. As you will see as we progress.

C major

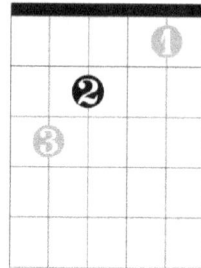

If you look at the A minor chord and then study the C major chord, they are very similar in the fact that you can get to the C major from A minor by just moving the 3rd finger from the third string to the fifth string.

Make sure you remember the string names. As it will help you to read chord charts quicker and figure out where chords are formed on the fretboard.

Once you have these four chords down (which shouldn't be too difficult) practice switching between them. Start with the E minor, go to E major, down to A minor, and then C major.

These are fundamental building blocks to playing rhythm, so make sure you know them well. Now let's look at it some more.

Lesson 9: G major & F major

The next two chords to learn are the G major and the F major. I chose the two for the specific purpose, that they can easily be switched to from the C major chord.

The G major chord is right above the C major and is also very common in songs. Two of the most common chords to play in a song are the G major and C major.

G major

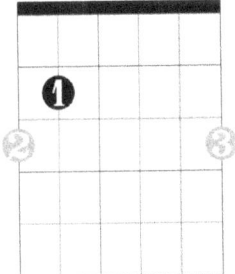

If you look closely at this chord, it's right above the C major chord. I present this chord here because it goes hand in hand with the C major chord.

Work at switching between these two chords. Because they are very common in a lot of songs. As you progress in your studies, you will see this more and more.

As you learn chords on the guitar, you want to work at switching between them as that is the essence of playing rhythm. Make sure to grasp this concept as it is vitally important.

The next chord to learn is the F major chord. I present this chord because it is right below the C major chord. When you compare the two chords, they are very similar.

F major

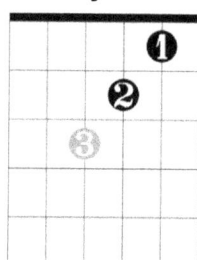

Can you see what I mean by these two chords being similar? If you play the C major chord and just move your third and second fingers down a string you'll form the F major. And the index finger doesn't even need to move.

This is the reason why the C major chord is a foundation chord. Because you can get to these other chords from it quite easily. You can go to the A minor, G major, and F major chords quickly and easily. That is of course if you practice.

Lesson 10: Chapter 2 Quiz

Here I present you with a quiz for chapter two. This a simple test to make sure you have learned the chords presented and know them well.

Remember, these quizzes are for your benefit. To make sure you learned the lessons and have retained the information.

Q: What is a chord chart?

A: _____

Q: What do the vertical lines represent in a chord chart?

A: _____

Q: How are the horizontal lines represented in a chord chart?

A: _____

Q: Why is it best to learn how to read chord charts?

A: _____

Q: What is the very first chord you learned in this chapter?

A: _____

Q: What finger needs to be added to make it a different chord?
A: _____

Q: What are the next two chords learned in this chapter?
A: _____

Q: Why is the C chord a foundation type of chord?
A: _____

Q: What chord is right above the C major chord?
A: _____

Q: What chord is right below the C major chord?
A: _____

Q: How many major chords are taught in this chapter?
A: _____

Q: How many minor chords are taught in this chapter?
A: _____

This chapter on chords will set up your foundation. So if you don't know an answer, go back and find it and write it down. This will help you to fully understand it.

Chapter 2 Summary

In chapter two we have learned about building a solid foundation for playing rhythm guitar. We learned about chord charts, how to read them, and a few fundamental chords.

Learning how to read chord charts can be very beneficial to you. It allows you to see how chords are shaped so that you can quickly form them, as well as enhance your musicianship.

But for this to happen, you need to work with them. Over time the chord shapes will stick in your mind and you will be able to recognize them easily and form them quickly.

These first few chords are very popular in songs and they are easy to transition into from previous chords. That is why they are chosen first to start building your chord vocabulary.

When going through your chords, start with the E minor chord as it is the easiest to form. Then progress through them in the order presented. Make sure to look at the chord charts to get the chord shapes firmly in your mind.

Forming chords, in the beginning, is not easy. Your muscles need to develop. So give it time. Have fun with it and take breaks when needed. Develop patience and you'll see results.

28

Chapter 3 More Chords

Lesson 11: D major & A major

Okay, now we're going to look at a few more chords that are common in songs. These will help to expand your musical foundation and chord vocabulary.

D major

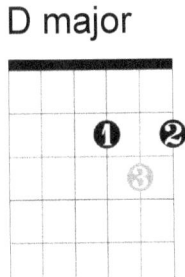

The D major is a triangle-shaped chord and a bit difficult to get to from the other ones presented so far. It is located on the first three strings on the first three frets.

It is very popular in songs and should be committed to memory. Once you learn it, try to switch between it and the other chords you have learned so far.

Now we come to the next chord in this chapter, the A major chord. Another chord that

A major

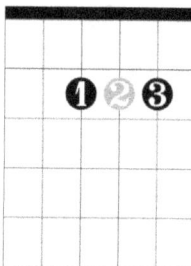

The A major chord is great because it is formed on the second fret on the second, third, and fourth strings. The only downside is that it's hard to get all your fingers on one fret.

People sometimes just bar this chord with one finger. That is an option too if you'd like, but it's a bit difficult as well. Just do the best you can with forming the chord.

You can also use your middle, ring, and pinky fingers to form the chord. Learning different ways to form chords will help you out in the long run. As you never know what chord will come next in a song.

That's what's great about learning to play the guitar, is that it is a journey of self discovery. You not only learn things about the guitar, but you also learn things about yourself.

Over time you will discover things that work for you better than others. You will begin to develop your style and bring out your personality through your playing.

Lesson 12: B minor & D minor

The next chord we'll learn is the B minor. Now, there are many different ways to play this chord, but we are going to learn the easiest way to play it.

B minor

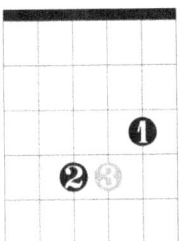

If you notice, this chord is the same shape as the A minor chord. It's just located two frets up from it. Which means, going back and forth between the two is easy.

You will also see this chord pop up from time to time in songs. So, forming it and playing it like this will make it easy to get to when it's needed.

Work on switching between the A minor and B minor chords. Along with switching between the Em to B minor. Make sure to add this chord to your vocabulary. That way when it shows up in a song, you'll be ready for it.

We now come to the next chord learned in the training, the D minor chord. This is the counterpart to the D major chord we learned earlier.

D minor

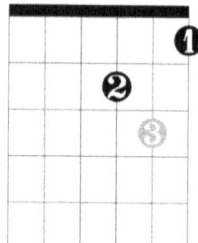

If you look closely at this chord, you'll see that we just move one note back a fret to create the minor counterpart to the major. Later I'll explain why this particular note.

Now, you will have to rearrange your fingers though to form it. But it is another popular chord to know. This chord will also pop up in a song from time to time.

It's not quite as popular as the D major, but it is popular enough that you will come across it from time to time. So make sure to add it to the minor chords that you have learned so far.

Remember, it will take a while for your hands and fingers to get used to forming and playing chords on the guitar. But with daily practice of going through them, over time it will get easier. Then that's when the real fun begins to happen.

Lesson 13: A sus2 & D sus2

Now that we have learned some of the basic chords that are popular in songs, we'll look at a couple more. These two have weird names but are very easy to form as they only require two fingers. A sus2 & D sus2.

A sus2

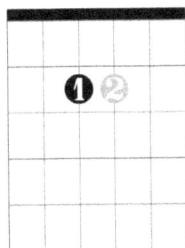

Here we have an A minor chord minus a note. We've moved the note back two frets to create the A sus2 chord.

This chord can be formed by just taking a finger off when forming either the A minor or A major. Can you see how easy it would be to form these three chords?

Play your A major chord. Then play the A minor, then play the A sus2. As you can see, these three chords are all right in the same area. This makes them easy to form and switch to within a song quite easily.

We now come to another sus2 chord. The D sus2. Once again, don't worry about the name, just the chord shape.

D sus2

Once again we take a note away from the D major, or D minor and we create a new chord. The D sus2 chord. This is another chord you'll see pop up in songs from time to time.

Now, do the same thing with this chord. Play the D major, switch to D minor, and then switch to D sus2. Like the A, these chords are all in one area and easy to switch between.

As I said, don't worry about the name of the chord right now. Just learn how to form it and remember the name. I will explain more when we get to the chapter on chord theory.

All these chords that you have learned in these three chapters are going to give you an excellent foundation for playing rhythm. And reading chord charts will help you improve your musicianship tremendously.

Here are all the chords learned so far:

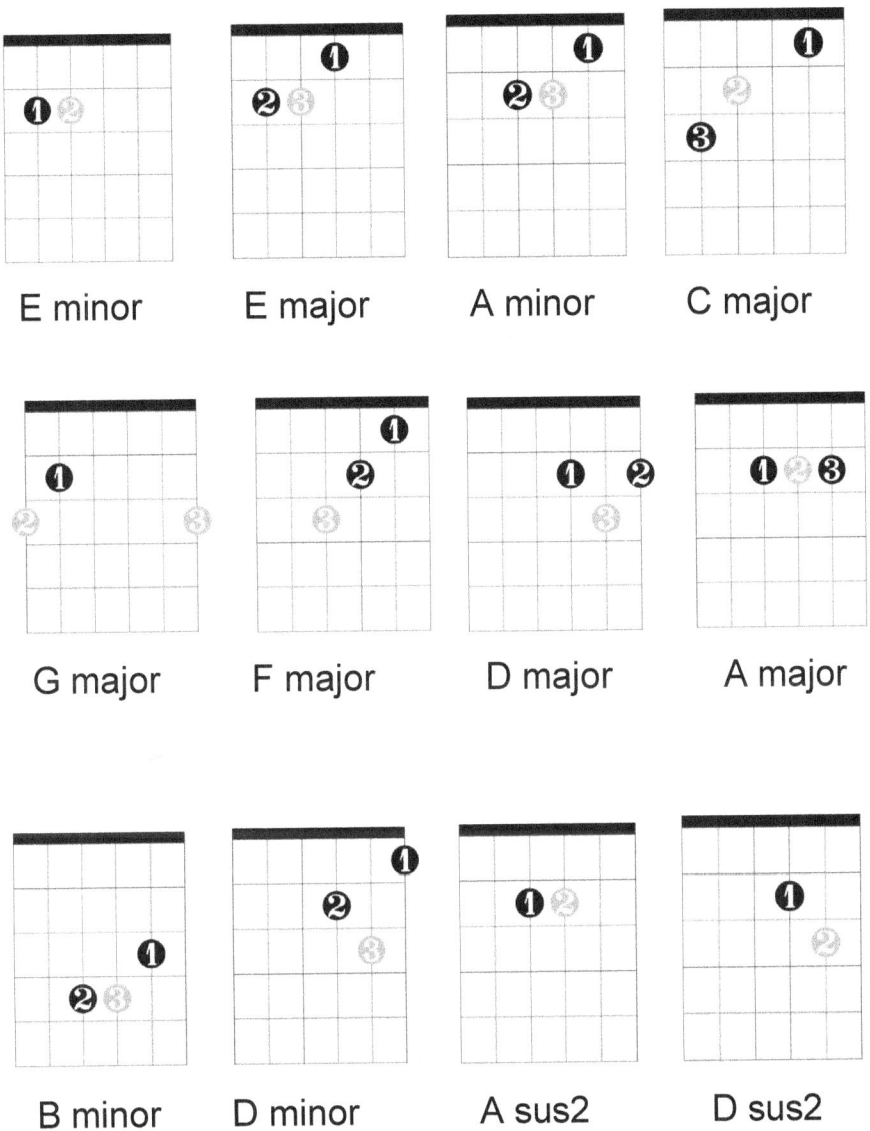

E minor   E major   A minor   C major

G major   F major   D major   A major

B minor   D minor   A sus2   D sus2

Review these twelve chords and know them all well.

Look at these twelve chords that we have learned so far. These will be your fundamental chord vocabulary. Notice how some of them are very similar. This will make them easier to play.

Also, notice that some are similar in the fact that they just move a note, add a note, or take a note away. This is how you create additional chords. By mastering the location of the notes.

Notice how C major and F major are very similar. How E major and A minor are as well. Notice how the chord A major just moves a note to create the A minor chord.

Notice how the A sus2 is created by taking a note away from the A major. Same thing with the D sus2 chord. You just need to take a finger off the fretboard to create this chord.

In reality, you're not taking a note away, you're just moving it to create another note. By knowing your notes, or knowing where to put your fingers, you create different chords.

When it comes to playing rhythm guitar, you must master chords. How to form them, change them, and how to create emotion with them when playing music.

This is the essence of being a great rhythm guitarist.

Lesson 14: Guitar tablature

Another type of sheet music designed for the guitar is called tablature. The standard type of music notation is designed for all instruments. As where tablature is specifically for guitar.

This type is a little bit different in the fact that it faces sideways like we play the guitar. Not upwards like in the chord charts. So I think it makes a bit more sense.

Here's an example of guitar tablature:

As you can see, we have only horizontal lines. These will represent the six guitar strings. With the low E (your biggest string) being on the bottom.

The strings are upside down from your guitar. The reason for this is that the lowest note is always on the bottom.

You'll need to remember this as it will make a huge difference in reading it. I didn't design it, I just teach it. But since it is designed this way, it'll take a bit of time to process.

When reading the tablature, the notes will be represented by fret numbers on the strings. This will allow you to spend more time playing and less time trying to figure out symbols.

So for instance, if you had a 2 on the top line, that would indicate the 2nd fret on the high E string. If you have a 7 on the bottom line, that will indicate the 7th fret of the low E string.

If you play a string without putting a finger on a fret, that will be indicated by a 0 on that particular string. A chord will be indicated by numbers stacked on top of each other. Or numbers that are written at an angle.

C major   C major

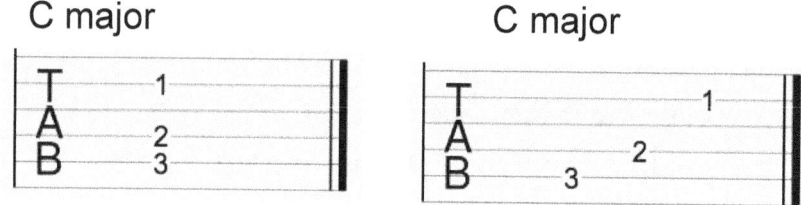

Here is the C major chord written in two different ways. When you play the notes together it's indicated by the numbers being stacked. Played individually, they're staggered.

Here are the other chords in tablature format:

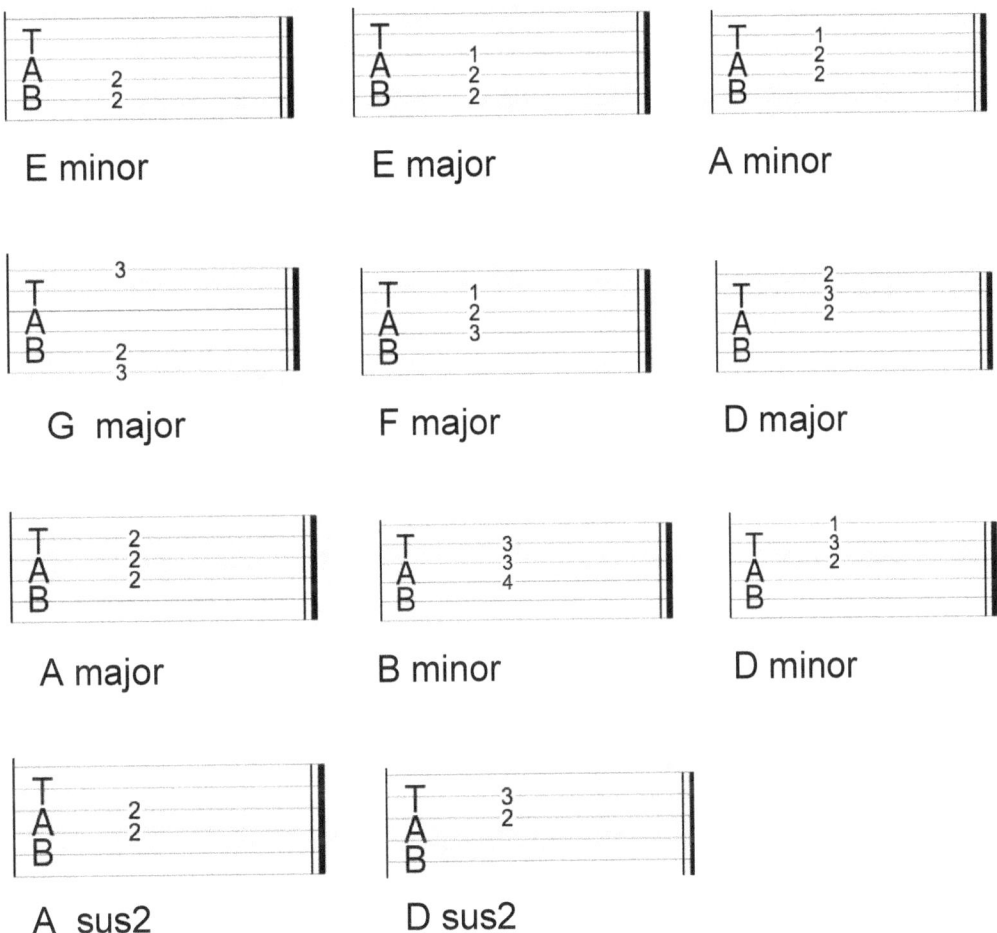

Remember, the strings are upside down. With the Low E string on the bottom. I know it doesn't make sense from a visual point of view, but if you take some time to study the way it's written, it eventually will. It will greatly benefit your guitar playing.

Lesson 15:   Chapter 3 Quiz

In this chapter, we have learned a few more things that will enhance our musicianship. A few more chords as well as another type of sheet music. Tablature. This with chord charts and you will be ahead of the crowd.

Q: What is guitar tablature?
A: _____

Q: What do the vertical lines represent in tablature?
A: _____

Q: What do the horizontal lines represent tablature?
A: _____

Q: How does tablature differ from chord charts?
A: _____

Q: What major and minor chords are taught in this chapter?
A: _____

Q: What sus2 chords are taught in this chapter?
A: _____

Make sure to study how to read tablature. It will be a huge benefit to you as you progress in your studies.

Chapter 3 summary

In chapter three we have learned a few more chords to add to our vocabulary. Plus a new chord type, the sus2 chord. I'll explain more about this in the chapter on chord theory.

We also learned a new form of reading sheet music that is a bit different from the chord charts we learned earlier. This form of sheet music is tablature.

Tablature is a form of sheet music designed specifically for guitar players. And if you learn to read it, it will not only help you with learning and writing songs but also improve your overall musicianship.

Most guitar players learn and play by ear. That's a great skill to have. And as time goes on, you will develop your ear to hear better as well. But don't overlook the written word.

If you take the skill of reading sheet music like tablature and mix it with playing by ear, you then have a very professional combination of skill sets. Which will make you a better guitarist.

Then, if you add in some basic understanding of music theory and how to form chords, you'll truly become a very proficient guitar player who can accomplish a lot in the music field.

Remember, all these chords can be found in a lot of popular songs. So make sure to learn them and learn them well, as they will be tools that will work for a wide variety of applications.

Make sure to study and get familiar with the shapes of the chords. Notice how some are very similar to others. This will make them easier to remember and use when needed.

Be sure to be able to read them in both chord charts and tablature format. Most people lean toward reading one or the other when it comes to chords. Learn to read both.

Remember what string you are on and what fret when reading the chord chart. Remember, the low E string will be to the left, but in the tablature, it will be on the bottom.

Reading the sheet music, forming the chords, and switching between them will all help to develop your fretboard hand. Not to mention eye-hand coordination. So work on this every day for the best results.

Chapter 4 Playing Rhythm

Lesson 16: The infamous guitar pick

Now that we know how to form chords without our fretboard hand, we want to learn how to bring them to life. This is done through the development of the picking hand.

The most common way to create rhythm with the chords is to strum them. This will be done by strumming across the strings while forming and switching chords.

One hand is forming and switching chords while the other hand is working on creating a rhythm and bringing the chords to life. This is where hand-to-hand coordination is developed.

To develop the picking hand, we first need to learn about the infamous guitar pick. This little device will allow us to get a nice pronounced sound out of the chords as we strum across the strings.

Here is an example of a guitar pick:

Now that we know what it looks like, we need to learn how to hold it. This will give us a chance to get the most out of it when we use it for playing rhythm guitar.

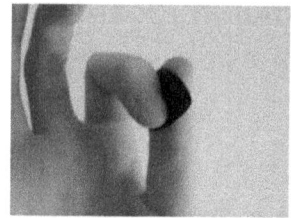 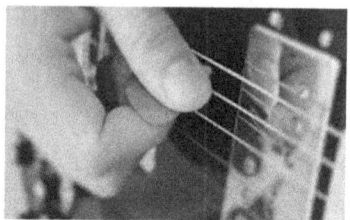

Here are two pictures that show how to hold the guitar pick, and how to use it when playing the guitar. Make sure to study these pictures and apply the pic as such.

You want to position the pick between your thumb and index finger as shown in the picture. Some people use the thumb and middle finger, but I recommend doing this way as it is most common.

Once you have it firmly grasped in your hand, bring it close to the strings and use it as it's shown in the other picture. Have the point facing the strings and hold most of the pick in your hands to create less friction.

Guitar picks are great because they come in all different sizes, shapes, thicknesses, and colors. I recommend you try out a few different ones until you find what works best for you.

This will take some time, but be well worth the effort.

Lesson 17: Strumming chords

Now that we have the guitar pick figured out, we can look into what it takes to bring all the chords to life by learning about rhythm. The most common way to create rhythm is by strumming the chords.

Remember, your fretboard hand will form the chords, and your picking hand will provide the rhythm that brings them to life. By mixing the two, you will create music.

By using a guitar pick instead of your fingers, you will produce a more pronounced sound out of the chords. The best way to do this is by strumming them. You pick across all six strings.

Strumming down: Quarter notes (count 1)

```
       G              C              D              G
 ┌─────────────┬──────────────┬──────────────┬──────────────┐
 T             │              │              │              ┃
 A             │              │              │              ┃
 B             │              │              │              ┃
 └─────────────┴──────────────┴──────────────┴──────────────┘

   D D D D      D D D D      D D D D      D D D D
```

Strum down four times on each chord. Strum evenly and at a steady pace. Listen to how it sounds like music.

Try strumming downward with other chords in the same fashion. Since everyone plays differently, you'll have to decide what tempo you want to play at. But make sure to keep it steady.

Strumming down and back up: Eighth notes (count 1 &)

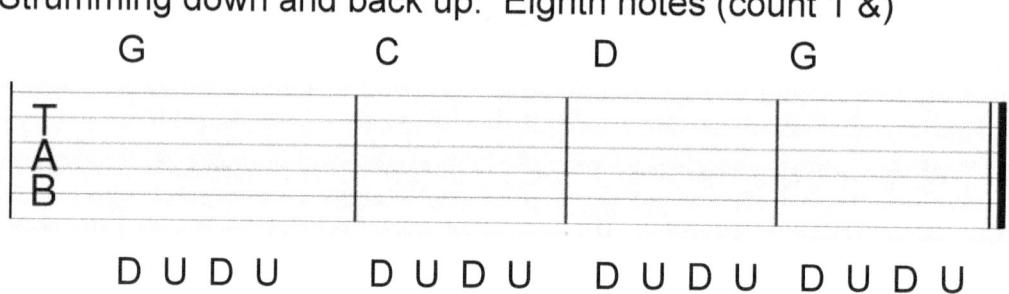

This example shows the same thing except you now strum back up on every other beat. Down, up, down, up, etc. This will help further develop the picking hand.

Strumming three notes at a time: Triplets (count 1 & uh)

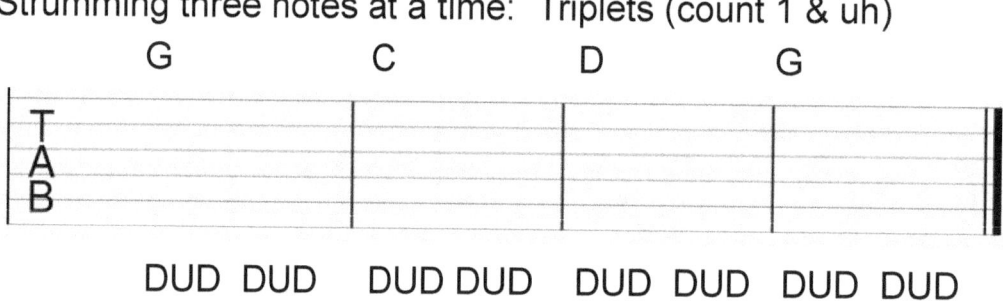

This example shows three notes strummed altogether. This will provide another type of rhythm. Practice these three strum patterns as they will provide you with a nice strumming foundation for many songs.

Lesson 18: Arpeggiating chords

After you get a handle on strumming chords, you can then work on learning about arpeggiating chords. This is where you play the notes of the chords individually. This approach will give you a different type of sound.

Arpeggiating chords have been around for hundreds of years and are associated with many styles of music that use stringed instruments. From Rock, to Jazz, to Country, and Bluegrass. A great way to help develop your picking hand.

This will give you a much softer sound than strumming as well as allow you to use your fingers in this style later on if you choose to do so. This will also give you more options as to what kind of rhythm you can produce.

Here is an example of how an arpeggiated chord reads in tablature format.

C

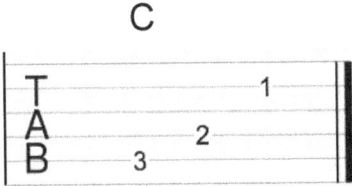

48

When reading chords that are played in this manner, take note of how they are written. When the notes are played together as in strumming, they will be stacked on top of each other. When they are arpeggiated, they'll be at an angle.

Here is another example:

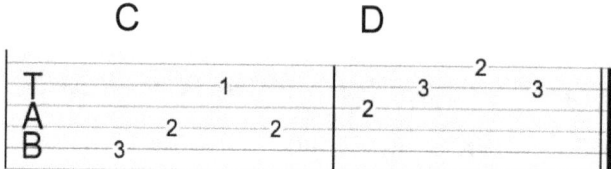

Here we have the C major chord and the D major chord. Both are played in the arpeggiated style. When playing the C chord you'll skip a string on the last note. This will provide a nice string-skipping exercise to help develop your picking hand.

The D major chord will be played in the same manner. Starting with the third string and progressing through the second and first. Each note of the chord is played individually.

Listen to how this approach gives you a completely different sound than when you strum the chords. Look at how it reads differently in the tablature as well. Being able to decipher the difference will help improve your musicianship.

This style of playing does require some discipline as the chords need to be formed on the tips of the fingers to allow the other strings to ring freely when picking them individually.

This technique will also allow you to develop discipline in your picking hand. When you work at picking the strings individually, you become a much better chord player as well as a rhythm player.

Watch for the notation. Notice how you ascend and descend the individual strings within the guitar chord. Choose any chord you like and pick the strings individually up and down. Listen for how it sounds.

As you do this, you'll begin to hear bits and pieces of songs that you recognize. Many popular songs use arpeggiated chords in them. So this will be a good technique to master for learning songs, as well as writing your own.

```
        Am              C              D
                                                      2
 T            1                   1    3     3
 A         2     2            0
 A       2              2
 B                 3
```

Here is an example of three chords all arpeggiated. Go through these chords and listen for how they sound compared to strumming them.

Lesson 19: Chord Progressions

Now that we know what chords are, how to strum them, and how to arpeggiate them, we can learn about how to put them together to construct rhythm within a song.

A chord progression is a series of chords put together in a specific order. They are what make up the framework of most songs. As a rhythm guitar player, you will want to make sure that you fully understand this concept.

In this chapter, we will look at some basic chord progressions that will show you how they work. This will give you insight into songs that you may already know, as well as insight into how to create your own.

Chord progression #1

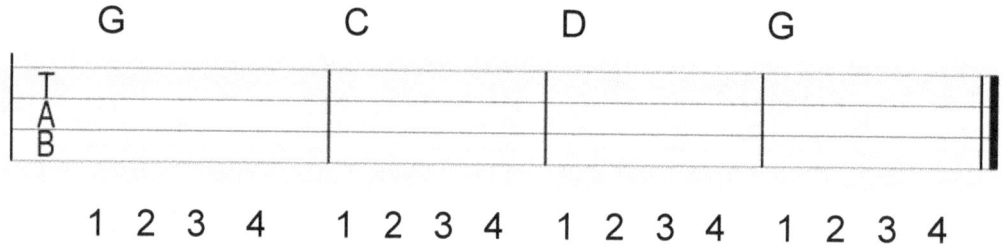

This is a very common chord progression. Either strum or arpeggiate the chords to hear how it sounds.

Chord progression #2

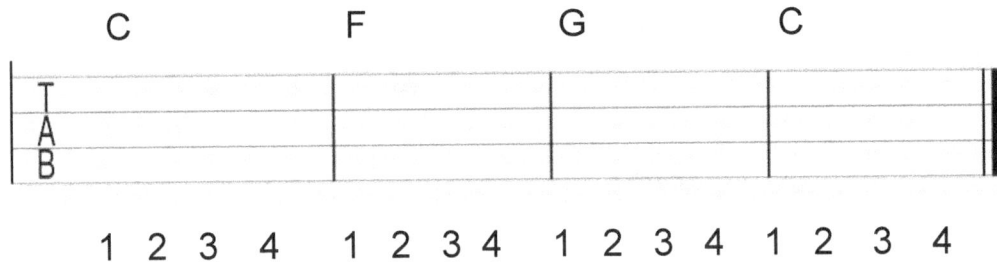

This progression starts with the C major chord instead of the G and switches out the D major for an F major chord.

Chord progression #3

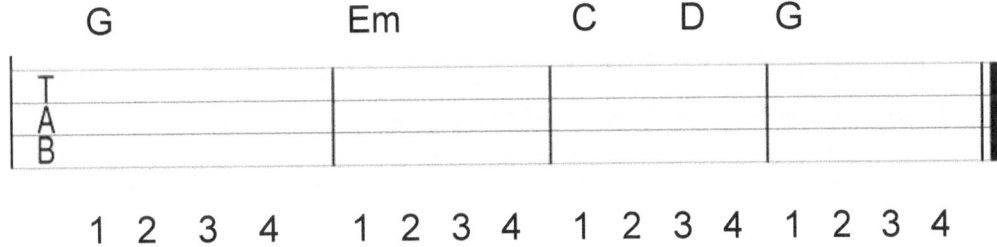

In this example, we add two things. One, the E minor chord, and two, we play two chords within the third measure. Here each chord will play for only two beats. Listen to how this changes the rhythm.

Use these examples to create other chord progressions out of all the chords you've learned so far. You'll soon hear music.

Lesson 20: Chapter 4 Quiz

In Chapter 4 we have learned some very important techniques that are associated with the development of the picking hand. The infamous guitar pick, strumming chords, arpeggiating chords, as well as chord progressions.

Here I present another quiz to make sure you know the material inside and out. Very important for being the best rhythm guitar player you can be. Remember, if you don't know the answer, go back through the chapter and find it.

Q: What is a guitar pick?

A: _____

Q: What is the function of the guitar pick?

A: _____

Q: What does strumming mean?

A: _____

Q: Why learn to strum chords?

A: _____

Q: How many beats are played per measure?

A: _____

Q: What are the three common ways to strum chords

A: _____

Q: What does arpeggiated picking mean?

A: _____

Q: What is the benefit of arpeggiated picking?

A: _____

Q: Can you play with your fingers?

A: _____

Q: What chords are used in the first chord progression?

A: _____

Q: What chords are used in the second chord progression?

A: _____

Q: What's different in the third chord progression?

A: _____

Remember, the development of the picking hand is as important as the development of the fretboard hand. Because the two hands need to work in harmony to create music.

Chapter 4 Summary

In chapter four we have learned some very important techniques. These are what will be used to bring your chords to life and help you establish a rhythm.

You can either strum your chords or arpeggiate them. Both options work well and will give you a different type of effect. You then create chord progressions.

Remember, the goal is to develop both hands and get them to work in unison with each other. Your fretboard hand forms the chords, and your picking hand creates the rhythm.

First, you have the infamous guitar pick. This is a very important part of playing the guitar. They come in different colors, sizes, and shapes. Make sure you try out some different ones to find what works best for you.

Second, you have strumming. This is where you form the chord and play all the notes at once. This is done by strumming the pick across the strings.

Third, you have arpeggiated picking. This is where you for a chord and play the notes individually. This is done by picking each string separately. This gives a unique sound to the chord.

Fourth, you have chord progressions. This is where you take the chords you've learned and put them into a sequence. This creates the framework for songs.

Now, there is a lot more to it than that, but this is the foundation of playing rhythm. Remember, what you are learning in this training is how to develop a solid foundation.

By learning and mastering the fundamental principles of playing rhythm guitar, you create a foundation that all future learning can stand on. And this will enhance your musicianship as you continue to advance your education.

Make sure that you work on each hand individually, and then get them to work in harmony with each other. The better this is developed, the better you'll understand how music works.

Chord development, strumming, arpeggiating, progressions, and timing are all essential elements to becoming a great rhythm guitar player.

Be sure to work on these concepts daily with determination and discipline.

56

Chapter 5 Seventh chords

Lesson 21: The A7 and D7 chords

Another type of chord that is popular to play in songs are seventh chords. These are a bit different from the majors and minors that we've been learning and will give a different sound.

With these chords, we add a flat 7th note to the three note triad to create a sound all its own. That is why these chords are popular and should be added to your chord vocabulary.

 What does it mean to add the flat 7th?

It means we add the flat seventh note from the key the chord comes out of. This creates a new chord. A seventh chord.

Ex: Key of G major: G A B C D E F#
                      1 2 3 4 5 6 7

As you can see from the example above, the 7th note is an F# in the key of G major. The G major chord is made up of the 1 3 & 5 of the key. By flattening the seventh note and adding it to the chord formula, we create a new chord. A G7 chord.

When we flatten a note, we take it back by one fret. In this case, it becomes an F note. This is added to the G major.

By flattening the 7th note and adding it to the three note chord formula, we create a new chord. A dominant 7th chord. This is labeled a 7th chord. So in the case of the G dominant 7th, we'll just call it a G7 chord.

Now, to keep things simple we are going to look at the chord shapes and not all the notes in each key. But they all work with the same concept as the key of G major. Add the fat 7th note.

This will allow us to stay focused on practical application instead of theory. Chord theory will come later in the training. For now, let's focus on forming the chords.

Being able to form and play the chords is what we are learning at this stage in the training. So let's stay focused on that.

Now let's look at the A7 & D7 chords.

A7   D7

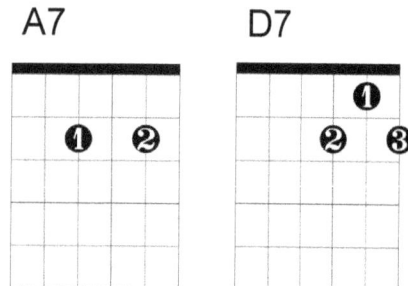

As you can see, the A7 requires only two fingers, and the D7 is like a backward D major. Simple and easy to form. This flat 7th note will create a different chord color.

Lesson 22: The C7 and B7 chords

The same thing goes with the C7 and B7 chords. They will allow us to create another shade of color. By flattening the 7th note within the key we can add to our chord vocabulary.

C7

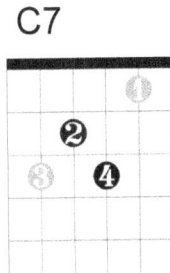

Look how we just add a note to the C major triad to create the C7 chord. By just adding a single note we get a different type of sound. Which creates a different type of mood.

By knowing what note to add and where it is located on the fretboard, you increase your knowledge of music.

Remember to always be looking at your chords in shapes. This will give you a visual picture to draw upon when you need to form the chord while playing.

Visualization is a big part of playing the guitar. As you progress with your studies, you'll see that everything can be broken down into patterns and shapes. Thinking like this will make it easier to learn and understand the instrument.

Now we come to the B7 chord. I like this chord because it is very similar to the D7 chord that we learned earlier.

B7

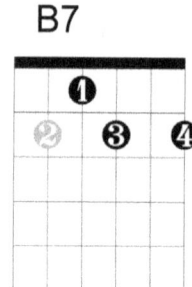

If you look closely at this chord, you can see the D7 shape in it. We just move it to the fifth string and add our pinky on the first string 2nd fret.

Here are a couple of 7th chord progression examples:

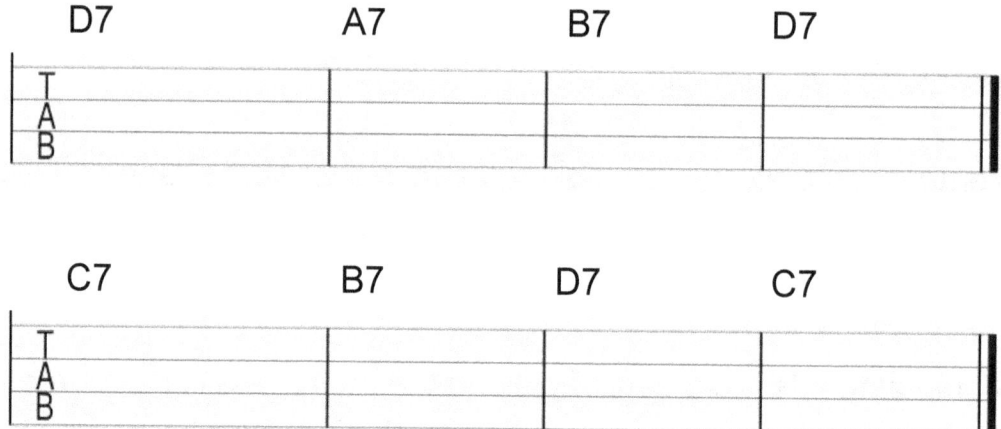

Use these to listen to how these chords sound different from their major and minor counterparts.

Lesson 23: The E7 and F7 chords

We now come to the E7 and the F7 chords. These are two more 7th chords to add to your arsenal of chords.

The more chords you have to work with, the more colors you can create. Remember, it is the flat 7th note that creates the dominant 7th chord. Which is just called 7th. As in E7.

There is no need to go into chord theory at this time, but it is nice to know why a chord is called what it is and how to create it.

E7

Here we have a chord similar to its major counterpart. If you look at the two, you can see that we just removed the note on the fourth string 2nd fret. It is this open D note that creates the flat 7th. Now we have an E7 chord.

Now the F7 chord is a bit harder to form. But can also be very useful in songs.

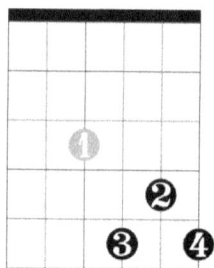

This chord has the D7 shape to it, but it is moved up to the 5th fret. We then add the F note that's on the fourth string 3rd fret. Since all four fingers are being used, this can be a bit hard to form. I recommend you practice it anyway.

Here are more chord progressions using 7th chords.

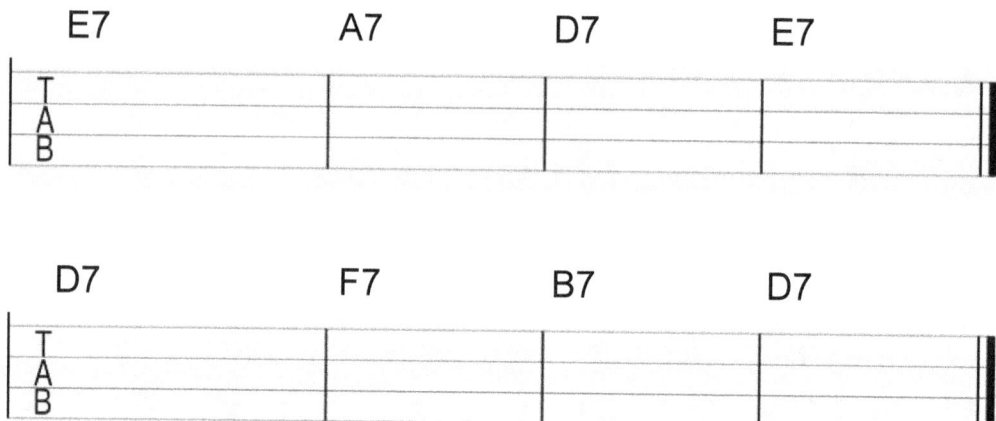

You can use any type of rhythm with these progressions. You can strum or arpeggiate the chords for different effects.

Lesson 24: G7 chord

Last but not least, is the G7 chord. This is one of the most popular 7th chords out of all of them. Once again it is fairly easy to form and will be a nice addition to the G major.

As you probably have heard by now (if you've been working with the chord progressions I've provided) the 7th chords offer a different shade of color. A different type of emotion, and as you continue to work with them, you'll recognize their sound.

G7

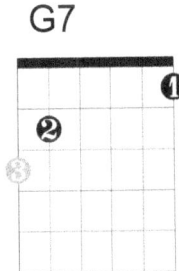

As you can see, this chord is very similar to the G major. But instead of the first finger being on the 3rd fret first string, it will be placed on the 1st fret of the first string.

The movement of just this one note will give the chord an entirely different sound. You will discover this as you continue to learn more guitar chords.

The addition, or subtraction of a note, can make a world of difference. And this is what you want to master.

As a rhythm guitar player, you want to have a nice toolbox full of guitar chords. And you want to be able to know how to form them. How to manipulate the notes to get different shades of emotion.

You want to be able to strum them as well as arpeggiate the chords. You want to look at chords as colors like an artist looks at paint.

Here are some more chord progression examples:

C7	F7	G7	C7

```
T
A
B
```

A7	D7	G7	A7

```
T
A
B
```

E7	D7	E7	D7

```
T
A
B
```

Lesson 25: Chapter 5 Quiz

In this chapter, we have learned a few more chords to add to your chord vocabulary. 7th chords. These are just a few of the most popular and will allow you to add additional color.

Q: What note added to the triad creates the 7th chord?

A: _____

Q: How many notes are in a 7th chord?

A: _____

Q: How many 7th chords are taught in this chapter?

A: _____

Q: What is the 7th note in the key of C example?

A: _____

Q: What kind of tone does a 7th chord produce?

A: _____

Q: What are the first two 7th chords taught in this chapter?

A: _____

Q: What chords are used in the first chord progression?

A: _____

Q: How many notes need to be fretted for the D7 chord?
A: _____.

Q: What strings are used to form the E7 chord?
A: _____

Q: What chords are used in the second chord progression?
A: _____

Q: How many notes need to be fretted for the F7 chord?
A: _____

Q: What strings are used to form the A7 chord?
A: _____

Q: How many notes need to be fretted for the G7 chord?
A: _____

Q: What chords are used in the third chord progression?
A: _____

Q: How many notes need to be fretted for the B7 chord?
A: _____

Q: How many notes need to be fretted for the C7 chord?
A: _____

Here are a few more things to remember about 7th chords.

The 7th chords are very common in songs.

The 7th chords are actually, dominant chords.

They are labeled 7th's as in A7, not dominant 7th.

The 7th chords are created by adding the flat 7th note.

The 7th chords are actually, considered dominant chords.

The 1 of the scale is the tonic and the 7 of is dominant.

The relation between the 1 and 7 creates tension in harmony.

These types of chords are good to know and use in music.
That is why they are so popular. They give you a different type
of emotional sound than the major and minor triads.

We can also create major 7th's by keeping the 7th note natural.
And minor 7th's by adding the flat 7th note to the minor triad.

Chapter 5 Summary

In this chapter, we have looked at a great way to add a new sound to the triad. This is done by adding the flat 7th note of the scale. This will create a dominant 7th chord.

The 7th chord is a very common chord type and must be added to your chord vocabulary. These chord types will allow you to create a different type of emotion than their major and minor counterparts.

By understanding how these chords are created and being able to find the correct note, within the key they come from, you will be able to increase your knowledge of music.

Don't forget that these chords can be easily formed if you know where your notes are on the fretboard. That is why it is vitally important to know your notes on each string.

The G7 chord just moves the note on the first string two frets down. While the D7 chord just flips itself backward from the D major chord.

Remember, the major 7th chord will just add the natural 7th note to the major triad, and the minor 7th chord will add the flat 7th note to the minor triad. All these chords will give you a well-rounded range of chord emotions.

What's great about the 7th chords is that they provide something different. A type of sound that is not major or minor, but a bit in between. This comes from adding the flat 7th note to the foundation chords.

Although they are technically called dominant 7th chords, most of the time they are just considered a 7th chord. As in G7, A7, D7, etc.

We create a new sound by extending the chord formula from a 1 3 5 to a 1 3 5 7, or 1 3 5 b7, or a 1 b3 5 b7. This allows us to create additional chords to add to our chord vocabulary.

But this can only be accomplished by knowing the notes within the key as well as where they reside on the fretboard. This will allow you to create endlessly. The more you know about chord construction, the better rhythm player you can be.

This is what basic chod theory is. Knowing the notes within a key or scale, and then being able to create majors, minors, 7ths, etc out of those notes.

Take time to study this concept and fully understand how chords are created. You can then begin to create different shades of color that will allow you to create different shades of emotion.

70

Chapter 6 Barre Chords

Lesson 26: Root 6 barre chords

Barre chords are the type of chords you use when you play further up the neck. The type that requires you to barre across multiple strings.

The most common are the root 6 barre chords. This is where the 1 or root of the chord resides on the 6th string. That is why it is called the root 6 barre chord.

Rt 6 G major barre chord

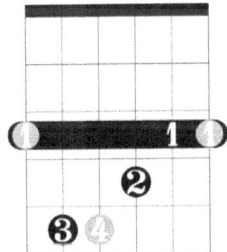

Here we have a root 6 G major barre chord. If you look closely, you can see the E major chord shape in there. Since the G note resides on the 3rd fret of the sixth string, this is where we would play this chord.

To change it to a root 6 A major barre chord, we'd find the A note on the 6th string (fifth fret) and play the chord shape there.

The benefit to these types of chords is that they don't change shape like the natural chords that we've been learning. To change the name of the chord, we just need to move them up and down the fretboard.

The downside to these chord types is that it can be difficult in the very beginning to form the barre across all six strings with your index finger. This will take some time and practice.

Rt 6 G minor barre chord

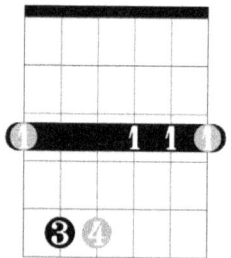

Here we have the root 6 G minor barre chord. As you can see it is very similar to the G major barre chord. We just take a finger off of the 5th fret third string.

Just like the natural E minor chord, we remove a finger from the major to form the minor. Here it is the same thing. Can you see the E minor chord shape in this chord?

This is where the root 6 barre chords come from. They come from the E major and E minor natural chords. When you move them further up the fretboard, you need to add the barre.

The reason for this is because the barre acts as a moveable nut. This is what your index finger represents. That is why when you form root 6 barre chords, you need to cover all six strings.

Like I said before, this can be a bit of a struggle at first. The index finger needs to cover all six strings which will create the nut, and the other fingers need to form the chord. Major or minor.

I recommend that you start with the root 6 barre first. Get your index finger to form the barre across all six strings and hold them down. This is the most difficult part of this chord.

Once you have that down (this will take some time, so be patient) then move the barre up and down the fretboard to different frets.

Once you have that accomplished, form the minor barre chord, and eventually the major. This will allow less stress on your wrists, hands, and fingers over time.

74

Lesson 27: Root 5 barre chords

Now we come to root 5 barre chords. These are very similar to root 6 barre chords except that the chords will be based on the 5th string instead of the 6th.

The reason for this is that the root note (the 1 of the chord) will be located on the 5th string. So this will make them root 5 barre chords.

The good thing about these chords is that you'll only need to bar across five strings instead of all 6. The reason for this is that the root of the chord (the 1) is located on the fifth string.

Root 5 B major barre chord

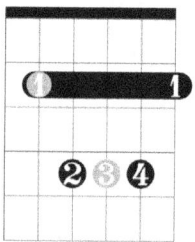

As you can see, the bar goes only to the fifth string. So this makes it a little bit easier to form and play. You bar with the index and form the chord (A major shape) with the other fingers.

Can you see the A major chord shape in this barre chord? The root 5 barre chords are built off of the A major and A minor natural chords.

Just like the root 6 barre chords are built off of the E major and
E minor, the root 5-barre chords will be built off of the A major
and A minor.

Root 5 B minor barre chord

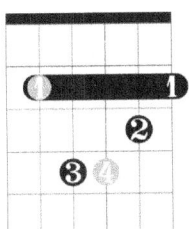

Here we have a root 5 B minor barre chord. As you can see,
the bar goes to the 5th string and the A minor chord resides
within it. Can you see the A minor chord shape in there?

Now, once we learn to form this chord, we can just move the
chord shape up and down the fretboard to play different chords.
We just keep the shape the same.

This is a B minor because the B note (root of the chord) is
located on the 5th string at the 2nd fret. If we moved it to the
5th fret of the fifth string it would become a root 5 D minor barre
chord. See how this works?

Lesson 28: Root 4 barre chords

By now, your index finger should be a little bit used to barring across the strings. Six strings for the root 6 barre chords, and five strings for the root 5 barre chords.

We now come to root 4 barre chords. These are a bit different. They are very similar to the root 5 barre chords in the fact that they use the A major chord shape. But they move up and down the fretboard as the barre.

Root 4 A major barre chord

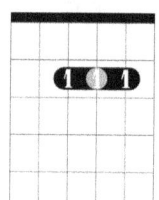

As you can see, this is very similar to the root 5 barre chord, except we are not using our index finger to barre to the fifth string. That's because the A note in this chord is on the fourth string 2nd fret.

Thus making it a root 4 barre chord. Get it?

Out of the three root barre chords, these are the easiest to play. But are normally only played in major positions. If you play the minor, then you normally would need to add the barre.

This would then turn it into a root 5 barre chord. Can you see how these two barre chords are very similar?

Root 4 C major barre chord.

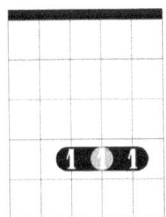

Can you see why this is a root 4 barre chord? Can you see why it's a C major barre chord? If not, let's take a look in more detail.

First, the C note (the 1 of the chord) like the B note in the previous chord is on the fourth string. Now, if you look closely, all we've done is move the chord shape up one fret. Since C is the next note, it becomes the name of the chord.

Remember, these chord shapes come off of the A major chord at the second fret. It changes the name as it is moved up the fretboard. Learn your notes and know the chord names.

Lesson 29: Timing sequences

Now that we have learned a whole bunch of chords, we want to look at timing sequences. This is where you create rhythm with the chords. We've discussed this a little before, but I want to discuss it more in detail here.

Timing is everything in music! Remember that. You can know all the chords and be able to switch between them, but if you don't have good timing, it won't sound like music.

At least not music that's appealing to listen to. So you want to make sure you pay attention to this lesson and get it down.

Timing sequences start with knowing your note values. Most Western music is divided into measures. The most common of these is a measure of music that contains four beats. This is sometimes called common time.

This is also recognized as 4/4 time. And within this time we have beats that have certain note values. We want to learn and understand these so we can apply them in our rhythm playing.

There are more than what will be described here, but this will be enough to get you started and on the right track to developing proper timing.

The six common note values that we want to master are whole notes, half notes, quarter notes, eighth notes, triplets, and sixteenth notes.

A **whole note** is a single note that will be played on the first beat and held for the other three.

A **half note** is a single note that will be played for two of the four beats.

A **quarter note** is a single note that will be played as one of a four beat measure. You count 1.

An **eighth note** is when you tie two quarter notes together. You count 1 and.

A **triplet** is three notes tied together. Here you count 1 and uh.

A **sixteenth** note is when you tie four notes together. The count for this will be 1 e and uh.

If you master these six time sequence note values, you will be able to create all kinds of cool rhythms in your playing. So be sure to do so.

Lesson 30: Chapter 6 Quiz

Here are some more test questions to make sure you fully understand what this chapter is teaching you.

Q: What are root 6 barre chords?
A: _____

Q: What are root 5 barre chords?
A: _____

Q: What chords do the root 6 barre chords derive from?
A: _____

Q: What chords do the root 5 barre chords derive from?
A: _____

Q: Why are barre chords so hard to play?
A: _____

Q: How does a root 4 barre chord differ from a root 6?
A: _____

Q: What does the index finger in a barre chord represent?
A: _____

Chapter 6 Summary

In this chapter, we have learned some basics about barre chords. These types of chords allow us to play further up the fretboard.

With the natural chords that we first learned, we stay around the first few frets. But with barre chords, we can now utilize more of the fretboard to create more sounds and emotion.

Remember, chords, chord progressions, and timing are the foundation for playing rhythm. The foundation for all song structure and creating something that is appealing to the ear.

Being able to apply this information to the fretboard of your instrument, will allow you to become a much better guitar player overall.

Study this chapter and make sure you fully understand the concepts I have taught you in it. They will help you to expand your knowledge of chords played further up the fretboard.

Remember, the barre chord is how you move chords up the fretboard. They can also be used to move down the fretboard. But they will take time to get used to so be patient.

The root 6 barre chord is made from the E major and E minor chords. We just move the chord shape up, and add the barre with our index finger.

The root 5 barre chords are made from the A major and A minor chords. Once again, we just move the chord up the fretboard and add the index finger to make the barre.

Root 4 barre chords are a bit easier to form as they only require the barre from the 4th string down. These are very popular in song. So make sure you work on mastering them.

Study your timing sequences. This is how you add rhythm to the chord shapes you've learned to create. Timing in music is everything. It is not enough to just know the chord shapes.

Remember, these are the fundamental principles of not just the guitar, but music in general. And they will come in very handy when playing with someone else, or a group.

Study, practice, and apply. Do this daily and you will see results. There can be no other way.

Chapter 7 Basic Chord Theory

Lesson 31: Notes of the Fretboard

In addition to learning practical application techniques and strategies as we have learned so far, we want to look into learning some basic chord theory.

In this chapter, we will start with the notes on the fretboard. This is essential to know if you are to work with creating and understanding the inner workings of guitar chords.

It all starts with the musical alphabet. The twelve notes that go from A to G#. A A# B C C# D D# E F F# G G#.
                 1 2 3 4 5 6 7 8 9 10 11 12

All these twelve notes reside on all 6 strings of the guitar. The string will determine what note you start with. But what is good to know, is that the notes always reside in the same order.

Let's look at the notes on each string.

84

Step 1. Memorize the notes of the open strings.

These are all 6 open strings. You tune the guitar to this. Make sure you understand this first.

Step 2: Memorize the notes on the Low E string

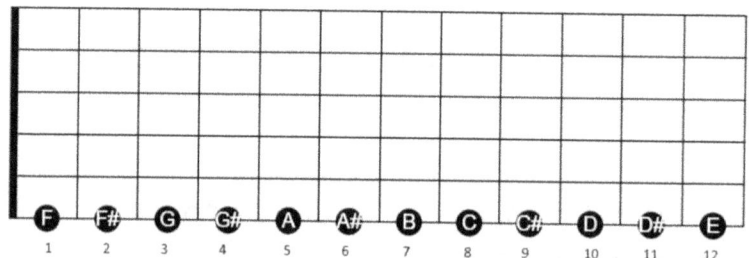

These are all the notes on the low E string from the 1st to the 12th fret. They repeat after that.

Step 3: Memorize the notes on the A string.

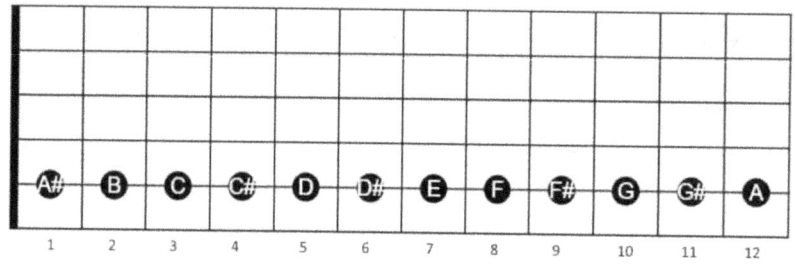

Step 4: Memorize the notes on the D string

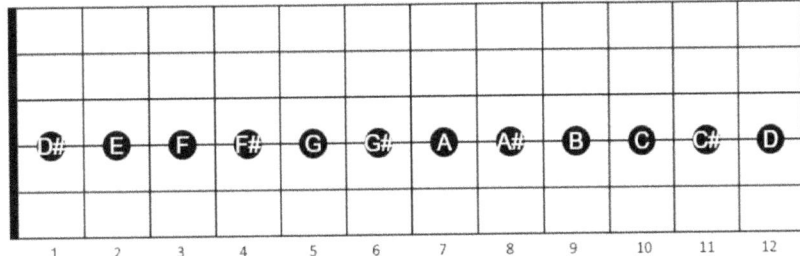

Step 5: Memorize the notes on the G string.

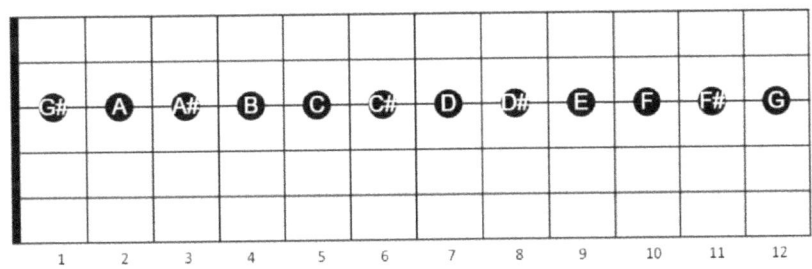

Step 6: Memorize the notes on the B string.

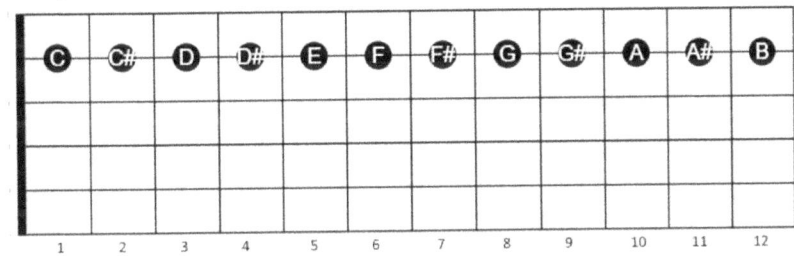

Notes on the high E string are the same as the notes on the low E string. So, you only need to memorize 5 strings. Be patient and take your time learning them. Knowing your notes will make you a much better guitar player.

Lesson 32: Major & minor triads

Now we know the notes on the fretboard, we can begin to learn how we use this information to figure out where to create the chords

A major triad consists of the 1 3 5 of the major scale. The minor triad consists of the 1 flat 3 5 of the major scale. So, if we want to create the major and minor chords, we simply find the notes in that scale to create it.

A major scale: A B C# D E F# G# A
                    1 2 3 4 5 6 7 8

The A major notes are A C# E. The 1 3 5

The A minor notes are A C & E. The 1 b3 5

Form these chords (which you already know) and then find the notes within the chords to see where they are located. Do this with all the major and minor triads that you have learned.

Remember, to turn any major into a minor chord, you flatten the 3rd note by one fret. Find it in each chord, and you'll be able to do this every time, with any major chord.

Lesson 33: Sus2 & sus4 triads

These chords are a great example of knowing your notes to create chords. You must know your notes to create different types of chords.

These are no exception. What I like about these, is that they play off of the 3rd note. Meaning, you just need to move the 3rd note forward or back to create them.

If you find the 3 of the major scale and move it back one fret it becomes a minor chord. If you move it back by two frets it becomes a Sus2 chord.

If you move the 3rd note forward by one fret it becomes the Sus4 chord. Thus changing the scientific formula for the chord shape. Yes, there is a science to this.

The Major: 1 3 5.   Minor: 1 b3 5.   Sus2: 1 2 5.   Sus4: 1 4 5.

Can you see how just moving one note can create a whole new chord? But to do this, you need to know your notes on the fretboard.

Learn your notes and your chord creation ability will be endless.

Lesson 34: Chord embellishments

Chord embellishments are where you add additional notes from the scale to create extended chords. Chords such as Gmaj6, Am7, Cadd9, etc.

All this means is that you are adding those particular notes from the scale to the triad. A Gmaj6 chord would be simply adding the 6th note in the scale to the G major triad.

The Am7 chord would be just adding the flat 7th note to the chord. If the 7th note in the A major scale is G#, we simply flatten it to G and add it to the A minor triad.

The same thing goes with the Cadd9 chord. It does exactly what it says it does, it adds the 9th note. Now, since there are only 8 notes on the scale, the 9 would be the same note as the 2 going into the second octave.

This is because 1 and 8 are the same note.

Some notes will need to be added, others will need to be flattened or sharpened and then added. Either way, this is how you can create thousands of chords and become a guitar chord guru.

Lesson 35: Chapter 7 Quiz

Basic chord theory is a great thing to know. Especially as a rhythm guitar player. Because you are going to be dealing with chords and how to get them to sound like music.

Q: What are the names of the six guitar strings?

A: _____

Q: What note is on the 5th fret of the sixth string?

A: _____

Q: What note is on the 8th fret of the fifth string?

A: _____

Q: What are the note formulas for the major & minor triads?

A: _____

Q: What are the note formulas for the Sus2 & Sus4 chords?

A: _____

Q: What are chord embellishments?

A: _____

Q: Why is all this information important to know?

A: _____

Chapter 7 Summary

In this chapter, we have looked at the basics of guitar chord theory. It all starts with knowing the notes on the fretboard. Once you get that down, you can create any chord you want.

Then you start with the major and minor triad. These are your foundation chords. Know their scientific note formulas and where these notes are in the chord.

Then you move the 3rd note either up one or back two and you create the infamous sus chords. Sus2 and Sus4. Also, triads that consist of three notes.

Once you have that figured out, you can add to them even more with chord embellishments. Which is basically when you add additional notes from the scale to create extended chords.

If you study these concepts with all the chords you've learned so far, you'll find that knowing the notes on the fretboard will open up a whole new world to you.

But to do so, you must study and apply the principles daily. This will allow you to get the most out of them.

Chapter 8: Additional Lessons

Lesson 36: Switching chords easier

In this chapter, we are going to look at some additional things to focus on. One of the things that is most important, is switching chords easier.

Forming the chords is step one. Switching between them is step two. So you want to focus on step two once you get step one down.

Switching chords needs to be mastered. Because it creates the chord progression that the melody plays over.

Here are a few tips:

1. Start with switching between two easy chords that are the same. Like for example E major and A minor. These two chords are a great place to start because they are the same shape. Just on different strings.

2. Try switching between two chords that change shape. Like for example C major to D major. This will help you in developing your finger and hand muscles. Which is very important for playing guitar chords.

3. Work at stringing three chords together. A lot of popular songs are comprised of only three chords. And once you can master switching between them, you're well on your way.

4. Once you have three chords down, try adding a fourth. Most songs will throw in a fourth chord for a bridge, or to change up the rhythm of the verse. So make sure to add a fourth chord in as well.

5. Take breaks from time to time. This will give your muscles time to develop. Especially when playing barre chords. Although the shape stays the same, it is taxing on the fingers to hold the chord.

6. Relax and develop patience. It takes time to be efficient at forming and switching chords. No matter what kind they are (open, barre, etc) give the mind and body time to develop.

7. Last but not least, practice these things daily. The more you apply yourself. The quicker you will see results. Be consistent in your efforts and you will come out a winner.

Lesson 37: Learning to mute strings

One thing that is very important when it comes to playing rhythm guitar, is muting strings. This serves two purposes.

1. It gives you a more percussive sound. Which can be very useful in certain parts of a song.

2. It allows you to stop other strings you are not currently playing from ringing out and making unwanted noise. This is very helpful for chord clarity.

There are two ways to mute your strings.

1. With your picking hand. You do this by laying the palm of your hand over strings to give a percussive sound or reduce string vibration.

2. With your fretboard hand. You gently lay your fingers across the strings to get the same effect. Add percussion, or reduce string vibration for a clearer sound.

This is a technique that will take some time to master. You just got to work on it. As you do, you will find what works and develop the skills necessary to mute the strings properly.

Lesson 38: Finger dexterity exercises

The next additional lesson that I feel will help you in your guitar playing is learning finger exercises.

Here are a few that can help you in this area.

EX: 1. Use one finger per fret moving through each string.

```
      5  6  7  8
T |-----------------|              |                 |                 |
A |                 |  5  6  7  8   |                 |                 ||
  |                 |              |  5  6  7  8      |                 ||
B |                 |              |                 |  5  6  7  9     |
```

Ex: 2. Start at the same fret but change the pattern.

```
      6  8  5  7
T |-----------------|              |                 |                 |
A |                 |  6  8  5  7   |                 |                 ||
  |                 |              |  6  8  5  7      |                 ||
B |                 |              |                 |  6  8  5  7     |
```

Ex: 3. Use the frets closer to the nut.

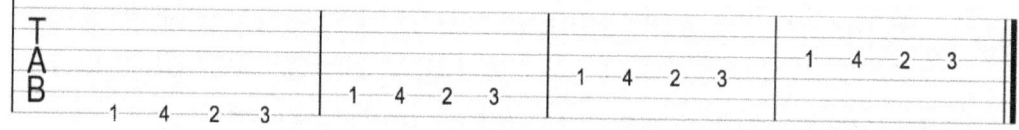

```
T |                 |              |                 |  1  4  2  3     |
A |                 |              |  1  4  2  3      |                 ||
B |                 |  1  4  2  3   |                 |                 ||
     1  4  2  3     |              |                 |                 |
```

In this last one, you'll have to do some stretching. But this will help to develop finger independence as well as dexterity in the fingers. Practice these daily for the best results.

Lesson 39: Developing practice habits

This lesson right here is going to make all the difference in your playing. Developing practice habits. Quality practice habits will keep you motivated and on track to your goal of becoming a great rhythm guitar player.

Here are some habits to develop and practice daily:

1. Set a goal, write it down, and put it where you can see it every day. This will help you to stay on track.

2. Start with finger exercises to get your hands and fingers warmed up. Very much like an athlete.

3. Go through all the triads that you have learned in this book. Major, minor, sus2, sus4, diminished, and augmented.

4. Work on picking hand development. This is how you bring the chords to life. The more you work on this the better guitarist you'll become.

5. Last but not least, work on the timing and theory that you have learned in this training.

Do all this daily and be consistent.

Lesson 40: Chapter 8 Quiz

Once again we have a simple assessment exercise (or quiz) to make sure you know the material in this chapter.

Q: What is the first lesson learned in chapter 8?
A: _____

Q: What do muting strings mean?
A: _____

Q: What do you accomplish by doing finger exercises?
A: _____

Q: What are some practice habits mentioned in this chapter?
A: _____

Q: What are these additional lessons so important?
A: _____

Q: Why is it important to have a goal and write it down?
A: _____

Like before, if you don't know the answer, that's ok. Just go back and find it, Study, practice, and progress forward. Do this daily and there is no way you cannot improve.

Chapter 8 Summary

In this chapter, we have looked at some additional lessons that can help you move forward in the quickest way possible.

But for you to do that, you must apply what you have learned daily. Just like all the other lessons in this training.

You start with finger exercises. Do these daily to keep your hands, wrists, and fingers in shape. This is very important to build strength and stamina.

Work at chord switching. This is essential for playing rhythm guitar. The better you can do this the more fluid your playing will be.

Learn to mute the strings to create a percussive sound when needed. As well as for controlling the vibration of unwanted strings.

Last but not least, develop good solid practice habits. This will determine if you become a good guitarist or a great guitarist. You will have to decide. Hopefully, it will be a great guitarist.

But like I've said before and will say again and again and again, you must apply what you have learned daily.

98

Learn To Play Rhythm Guitar Conclusion

If you've made it this far I congratulate you on your accomplishments and say "Thank you for your purchase of this book and your time learning to play the guitar". You seem like the kind of student that I'd love to teach in person.

This training has taught you many things about playing rhythm guitar, and you should now be well-versed in many concepts and techniques related to it.

As well as a basic foundation of music in general. But to fully understand it all, you need to study, practice, and apply what you have learned. This can only be accomplished through commitment and daily effort.

All that you have learned in this training guide will provide you with a solid foundation of rhythm guitar playing. Does it teach you everything? No, but it provides a framework that can be built on with further studies.

When it comes to playing the guitar, there is always more that you can learn. The better your foundation, the quicker and easier future learning will develop. And that my friend, is where the fun comes in.

You are learning skills that can last you a lifetime and allow you to pass on to others if you choose to do so. Remember, it takes time to accomplish anything, and anything worth doing is worth doing right.

Remember also, that music is a language and there is a learning curve just as with any other type of language. So be patient and give it time to develop. One small step at a time in the right direction will produce amazing results.

If you find value in this book, please do let me know by leaving a review. Or, if you have any questions about any lessons in the book, be sure to let me know that as well. I will be happy to assist you.

Be sure to follow me on Instagram, Facebook, etc. I am on just about every one of them out there.

Visit my website at DwaynesGuitarLessons.com

Best of luck and have fun.

Sincerely, Dwayne Jenkins
Tritone Publishing. copyright © 2023

Other Books By Dwayne's Guitar Lessons

Rock Guitar 101:

A beginner's step-by-step guide to rock guitar basics. A system of 7 lessons designed for someone just getting started and absolutely no previous musical knowledge is necessary.

7 quick and easy lessons that go through the fundamental principles that allow you to build a solid foundation and get ready for future study in the art of Rock Guitar.

Learn Guitar: Simple Method For Beginners:

Learn Guitar: Simple Method For Beginners has been created specifically for students with no previous musical background. With lesson examples presented in today's most popular step-by-step format.

If you're looking to learn guitar, no matter if it is rock, blues, or any other style and you're interested in either acoustic or electric, this book will help you get started.

Lead Guitar Wizardry Volume 1:

Lead Guitar Wizardry Volume 1 presents you with the fundamental principles and secret formulas necessary to become not only a lead guitar player but a lead guitar wizard.

Lead Guitar Wizardry Volume 1 is a comprehensive study guide on the inner workings of lead guitar playing. From finger exercises to picking techniques, scale patterns, and fretboard knowledge.

All books are authored and self-published by Dwayne Jenkins and can be found on Amazon.

These can also be found on Dwayne's website in digital format for quicker learning. Just download it onto your computer and start learning right away.

Online courses are also available with video instruction, assignments, and assessments to make sure you fully understand the material.

Self-study is a great way to learn as it allows you to not only go at your own pace but also develop the skills of discipline and time management. These things can benefit you in other areas of your life as well.

If more help is needed, Dwayne also offers one-on-one private coaching. Which can also be found on his website.

Also, be sure to check out Dwayne's video lessons on YouTube. These are free and available 24 hours a day, 7 days a week, 365 days a year.

About the Author

Dwayne Jenkins is a professional guitar teacher, an accomplished musician, and an entrepreneur. He has been learning, playing, and teaching guitar lessons throughout Denver, CO for over two decades.

He is now bringing his special training skills and methodology that have been honed and hand-crafted throughout the years on how to play to students around the world.

Dwayne has a unique exciting approach that gets students of all ages and skill levels enjoying the fun of playing guitar and ukulele. His enthusiasm and love for teaching shine through with every lesson that he creates.

His lessons are designed to enhance your ability to progress. No matter your reason for learning, there will always be something in Dwayne's books and products to help you achieve your dreams.

So if you're a student looking to start, or a student looking to further your education, be sure to get involved with Dwayne's guitar lessons and learn what so many people have already discovered why learning to play the guitar or ukulele, is one of the greatest things you can do for yourself

106

What Students Are Saying About Dwayne's Guitar Lessons

"Dwayne, thank you so much for everything you have taught me and done for me. You are an amazing guitarist and wonderful teacher" BJ

"Dwayne, it has been a true pleasure to have you at our house each week! Ken & Trevor have learned so much through you and your teachings. Thank you!" Lisa

"Dwayne, thank you for being a great teacher and teaching me many great songs. This is a skill that will last me a lifetime." Danielle

"Dwayne, we want you to know we are honored to have you at the studio. We appreciate all that you do and are grateful that we can leave you in charge" Angie & Wilson M.E.C

"Dwayne, we are so glad you are our Teacher. It's been three years already can you believe it? Thank you again. You're the best!" Chelsey & Lucas

"Dwayne, we are so glad that you are in our lives. Chelsey & Lucas enjoy their time with you and look up to you. Looking forward to another great year!" Love and best wishes, Ken & Sue.

"Dwayne, thank you so much for being not only an awesome guitar teacher, but an awesome friend as well" Kayla

"Dwayne, thank you so much for all the years of doing lessons. You have been very patient with my progress helped me to build confidence in myself and inspired me to follow my dreams. And in doing so you have become a great friend" Jake

"Dwayne, thank you for teaching Nick guitar so well. He loves it and is getting quite good fast. I'm amazed!" Jane

"Dwayne, Thank you so much for teaching me every Saturday and not only teaching me guitar but also about life and helping me with setting my goals. You are a great teacher, mentor, and the best friend ever" Carson

"There is not another person I would want to be teaching me a guitar! His 1 on 1 teaching makes learning guitar very personal & exhilarating. He teaches at your pace and takes pride in what YOU want to learn. The best part...if Dwayne doesn't know a song a student wants to play, he takes time out of the week to learn it His teaching comes to life in my performance and has progressed over the last 8 years. Words cannot describe how amazing a teacher, rockstar, and true friend Dwayne has become to me" Dominic